stratēchic

Life and Career Winning Strategies

for Women

D1409670

Michele Thornton

Mynd Matters Publishing

SECOND EDITION

Cover design by FourBlend
Photography by Adewole Photography
Logo design by Brittney Dorsette

ISBN: 978-0-9899164-2-4
Library of Congress Control Number: 20155920813

Printed in the United States of America

To my family, Tony, Taylor, and Jordan
You inspire me daily to want more,
be more, and do more.

Thank You!

Diana—

Many Blessings

Michele Hart

CONTENTS

ACKNOWLEDGEMENTS

This book has been a dream of mine for a long time. I knew I had a story to share that could benefit women across the globe. I have not always been Strategic and definitely not a Stratechic. I have been played, taken advantage of and just made bad decisions. What I know for sure is that all things are possible through God and that this is my story to share at this particular time in history. I also know that none of this would be possible without the following people: My heavenly Father who has blessed me and covered me with His almighty Grace! My dad, Walt Thornton, who was such an inspiration through his hard work as an entrepreneur and sales executive. I made a promise to him on his deathbed that I would make him proud of me. I hope that I've kept my word. My mom, Francoise, who sacrificed her dreams so that I could pursue mine. I am eternally grateful to her and I share this dream of writing a book with her. My brother, David, is my conscience. He is such a good man--a man of God. He has been on this journey with me as a reminder that I can do anything! I know what greatness and sacrifice look like because of my aunt, Dr. T's, commitment to education. I hope she knows her life has been an inspiration to me and all that I have achieved. Mamalene, my grandmother, who taught me to stand on my own, be independent and that you are never too old to know and love God. My husband, Tony, he inspires me everyday to be better, walk with integrity, give back like I may need someone to give to me one day and all of the other sacrifices he makes for me to do what I do! My Village – Joy thank you for always telling me the truth and encouraging me to be better! Nicole (Coco), the pepper to my salt, my light on this journey- you have given me unconditional love and friendship! As long as I have family- you have family. I will always have your back. What it do Coco. Tiffany R, Tiffany B, Stepp, Renee, Jackson, Bozoma, Shetellia, Lynn and Lyte. These are my Stratechics! Every woman needs a posse of supporters that will tell her the truth! Mike & Teneshia Warner (Egami Consulting) thank you for your direction & guidance on the strategy for *Stratechic*!!! Thanks to my hairstylist, Will Robinson, who did my hair for the cover and once a week to keep me looking right! I need to give a special shout out to Brittney Dorsette who encouraged me, created my logo, answered my phones and, most importantly, prayed for me along this journey! Last but not least, I want to thank Taylor and Jordan for their love and support. They remind me everyday that all things are possible.

If you don't build your dreams someone will hire you to help build theirs .

Quote by Tony A. Gaskin Jr.

PREFACE

"People are the most valuable known resource. The better they are crafted, the more valuable they are. Underutilized resources may result in greatness this world will never know. Waste Not, Want Not."
- Brittney Dorsette

Be an owner, not a renter. My boss and one of my advisors, Louis Carr, loves to remind his management team that in business, it's important to have an owner's mentality. Owners invest in their businesses and think long-term. Unlike renters, owners are fully invested and consistently give it their all. Renters rarely, if ever, give the same effort or attention to detail. Renting is temporary and focused on the short-term. In life, don't behave like a renter. Be an owner of your present and future. Invest in it. Be deliberate about what you do and how and with whom you do it. You must develop a plan; one you actually write down and implement.

Often, we read books that tell us to feel good, be empowered, or live your best life but don't give us a roadmap or a timeline to get it done. Unlike the aforementioned, **Stratechic** is a step-by- step framework for you to become strategic in your approach to be your best self. This will not happen overnight but through purpose, intention and practice you will become **Stratechic** about who you are and what you want!

INTRODUCTION

I grew up in Oakland, California. The daughter of two parents who worked hard, I had a good childhood. We weren't rich, but we weren't poor either. My parents sent me to decent schools and I was a strong B student as well as an athlete. I played basketball through my junior year of high school but losing my love for the game resulted in my not playing during my senior year. Choosing not to play was one of the primary reasons I didn't go to college right away. When I think back, I can admit to feeling like somewhat of a failure. My friends were all preparing to depart to different colleges and I didn't even fill out one college application. I was following the path of both of my parents, neither of whom went to college.

Shortly thereafter, I met a man and fell in love. You know the story. I began living for the next date or call that didn't come as often as I wanted. I was likely filling the void of not spending enough time with my father growing up. He worked seven days a week, fourteen hours a day. We rarely did much as a family and even less as father and daughter. My mom was the one constant in my life and I love her for it. This isn't to say my father was a bad person. However, it simply explains why I made certain decisions growing up.

At this point, I was a high school graduate, was in a bad relationship and still lived at home with my dad (my mom moved back to Montreal to care for her parents) with no future plans. On my 21st birthday, I decided something had to change. As fate would have it, later that year I was introduced to a successful guy who played in the NBA. We began dating and I finally realized why I was born: to be HIS wife. Just plain Crazy! Ladies, how many of you have decided what your own destiny looks like? I can tell you it's a very dangerous thing to invoke your own will. From the age of twenty-one through twenty-five, I lived my life through someone else's dreams and successes. I made sure I was available emotionally and physically for someone else's benefit.

I remember the precise moment I decided to walk in the destiny that was designed for me but I had been failing to grasp (not the one that I had manufactured, but the one I was actually born for). Clarity came when I realized I was not created to be arm candy, a side piece or whatever you would call a woman dating men because she doesn't love herself. I was operating in an adult world, dating through the lens of a young girl constantly seeking affection from men because of the void from a father's love—A father whose presence only lacked because he worked day and night to provide for his family.

I haven't told many people this. I was about twenty-five years old and extremely unhappy with my life and circumstances. I was in a horrible relationship, had no direction, and very little education. It was crazy because people would look at me and actually envy my life. One night, I had a dream. I was driving my boyfriend's Porsche across the Bay Bridge. The road was littered with potholes and I was doing my best to avoid them. Finally, I pulled over and got out of the car. When I stepped out, God was standing there in front of me. Although He didn't speak one word, I knew he was rightly disappointed in my choices and me. I dropped to my knees, cried and prayed, asked Him to change me and to change my life. When I awoke, I recalled every detail of the dream.

Shortly thereafter, I enrolled in school, my relationship ended, and I began to live differently. I made sacrifices. I no longer had financial support from a boyfriend. Instead, I took care of myself by cleaning houses and working at the front desk of a hotel. Unfortunately, I also gained thirty pounds because I didn't have time to make smart food choices.

Through it all, God had directed me. He whispered that there was something better for my life—a different path. We have to sacrifice and walk in the valley to appreciate the journey to the mountaintop. I haven't arrived, but I'm reassured that I will make it.

The essence of **Stratechic** is to remind and reaffirm that each of us can reach our mountaintop. We can overcome all setbacks and challenges to reach our goals. It won't always be easy but it will definitely be worth it! In this book, I share the 10 strategies that have made me a "Stratechic." I will also introduce you to the results of an in-depth 2015 Women & Strategy Research Study I commissioned via a third-party agency. The study was comprised of entrepreneurs, entertainers, wives, community leaders, business executives, stay-at-home moms, and everything in between. They are influencers within their homes, communities, networks, and organizations. While the majority may never wear the title of CEO, I've learned that most people who influence change don't require a title.

GREATEST THING THAT'S EVER HAPPENED TO ME

I've worked in the media and entertainment industry for the past fifteen years. In the past three years, I've been promoted to the senior executive team of my company as the Senior Vice President of Media Sales for Centric, "The First Network Designed for Black Women." There are very few women who lead media sales organizations and even fewer Black women lead in that capacity.

To continue to grow the revenue stream for our network, strategy is critical to our team operations. I quickly realized, once I put a strategy together for my life, everything improved both personally and professionally. My good friend Bozoma Saint John often uses the phrase "Let's Go!" She uses it to remind herself how important it is to get up when a personal tragedy strikes and knocks you down. She is the ultimate Stratechic. But I'm getting ahead of myself.

This is NOT a book for someone looking to simply feel good or feel empowered. This is NOT a book to get over a bad relationship. So many things in our lives are for, or because of, someone else. This book is a gift to us.

I've read that 80% of women don't ask for what they've earned. Not what they want, but what they've actually earned. I was at a women's conference and the facilitator asked us to participate in an exercise. We were directed to share with the people sitting next to us the best thing that's ever happened to us. The young lady sitting beside me went first as she was so excited to share her story. She had just given her grandfather a 75th birthday party. It took months to plan and it was a huge success. I was sitting there staring at her (hopefully not with my mouth open). It hit me like a ton of bricks that for most women, the best thing that happens to us is something we do for someone else. Please take a minute to digest this as it is a key point and the foundation for everything found within these pages. One of the best qualities we have as women is our giving and nurturing spirit. Stratechic is a manual for taking that God-given trait all women possess and leveraging it to begin our transformation into strategists. Let's make a commitment today that the best thing that happens to us is NOT something we've done for someone else.

The Greatest Thing That's Happened to Me Exercise (30 minutes):

Before we continue, I want you to put things into perspective and make a list of a) the greatest thing that's ever happened to you, b) the greatest thing you've done for yourself, and c) the greatest things you've done for others. Feel free to include several items within each list. My lists are provided below for guidance:

The Greatest Thing That's Ever Happened to Me:
- I'm a Wife and Mother
- I realized God loved me before I could love myself
- Self-Awareness became part of my daily habits
- I have unconditional friendships
- Received numerous awards from amazing organizations

The Greatest Thing I've Done for Myself:
- Moved to New York to work in the television business
- Love myself unconditionally
- Educated myself at 30 years old
- Understand that I'm the master of my happiness
- Not allow people to steal my joy
- Hired a voice and diction coach
- Learned to accept help from others

The Greatest Thing I've Done for Others:
- Cared for my dad during his bout with leukemia
- Support children and youth causes
- Tell people the truth at all times
- Raise money for various foundations
- Inspire and motivate others through my actions
- Create diversity opportunities for others in the media business

We often confuse the greatest thing that's happened to us with the greatest thing we've done for others. Let's un-blur the lines to ensure they are categorized appropriately in our lives. We MUST RECOGNIZE the things we do for others as just that. When we get Stratechic, we become more intentional about our time and energy. We think about them as investments. To whom or what are we investing our time? How much time and energy are we investing in certain people and activities? What's the purpose for which we are investing our time and energy to those people and activities? More importantly, we begin to understand the significance of doing things for ourselves because we deserve it. For many women wearing multiple hats and filling countless roles, if we don't do it for ourselves, it won't happen!

WOMEN & STRATEGY

If you have ever searched for books on women and strategy, you'd know the results are quite limited. I was disappointed but not surprised. Books are readily available on empowerment, love, fitness, finance, and leadership. I've found that strategy is a necessary tool for each of those topics and frameworks.

So what's the official definition of strategy?

Strategy: a careful plan or method for achieving a particular goal usually over a long period of time. [1]

Merriam-Webster's Dictionary states the first known use of strategy in 1810. However, other sources note origination in the 6th century as a military term. Generals instituted strategies to win wars and protect the world. Regardless of the source, there are no feminine connotations associated with the meaning of strategy—at least not in the definition's purest form.

Throughout these pages, I address strategy as it relates to women. Our common definition for strategy, in this sense, is when a woman carefully designs or plans to serve a particular purpose in her life and to capitalize on the qualities with which she was born. The beauty of being a *Stratechic* is   that you don't have to act or think like a man. You just need to use all the power and gifts you inherently have as a woman. Three common themes from the women's definition of "strategic" in the 2015 research study, were:

1. *Having clearly defined goals that you work toward*

2. *Having long-term vision and being intentional about planning*

3. *Not focusing too much on the short-term*

Let's break down those definitions.

The Simple definition of Strategic: *Carefully designed or planned to serve a particular purpose or advantage.*

The definition of **Stratechic**: *When "women" carefully design or plan to serve a particular purpose or advantage for their lives!*

Having this mindset is integral for all women. I consistently interact with women that are NOT Stratechics. They do not plan or design their future. They live like renters and not owners. They only plan their next outfit, vacation, job, diet, or boyfriend, but not an overall strategy for life. The dirty little secret is that women are born strategists. At a very early age, we have to learn how to manage the playground with other girls, manage group dynamics in middle school, and deal with all of the decisions around dating and what colleges to attend. Then, we grow up and have careers and families. I multitask on a daily basis to juggle the demands of career and family.

Everyone has a moment in his or her life that is life changing. It is a small voice gently urging you to follow a course putting you on a path to your destiny.

MOST OF US DO NOT LISTEN!

Stratechic is about learning how to course-correct your life. The lessons on these pages are designed to help you learn from mistakes and listen to that small voice whispering (and sometimes yelling) your name. The voice that only has your name and destiny in mind when it speaks.

This book doesn't just force you to think, it demands you to put those thoughts into action. A plan means nothing without execution! It means you have to create a strategy, a plan for you to live your best life. The good news is that women are born with all of the characteristics to be strategists. We just don't always take the time to tap into our inherent qualities. Or, we've gotten comfortable using our time and energy to help others live their best lives. In the words of Bozoma, *Let's Go!*

LESSONS FROM THE 4TH GRADE
(FROM MY DAUGHTER)

I've been contemplating writing this book for the last five years. I've always wanted to share what I've learned along the path of my life and career that helped me navigate Corporate America and better yet, life. Suddenly, there was one defining moment that clarified my path and direction. I knew I had to write a book on strategy when a fellow mom at my children's school told me that the strategies I was teaching my daughter would never work long-term. Isn't it amazing how things are born and become clear? All of the things I had experienced were crystalized in this one small exchange! I find it interesting that giving my daughter advice (she's ten) about loving herself and not letting others define her is called a strategy. I won't go into detail but I will say that I taught my daughter a valuable lesson my grandmother once taught me. "When someone doesn't want to share with you, acknowledge you, or tries to exclude you or diminish your being, you have the power to do things for yourself." That power means sometimes buying it for yourself so you'll never be at the mercy of anyone, whether it's in a classroom or boardroom.

Stratechic is designed to help women cultivate their female instincts to build a strategy for their lives. It is a call-to-action when people say you're not qualified, you won't win, you'll never graduate, you'll never get married or have a satisfying relationship, or you'll never fit into that size again. In truth, having a plan and executing against that plan is the best revenge for negativity. *Stratechic* will help you crystalize a path forward no matter your circumstances. The preparation is very personal for each of us but the foundation is the same. These are ten steps that will prepare you for any situation and help you towards becoming your "personal best." The attributes I present will prepare and fuel you for every good thing you want to happen.

This process takes planning, discipline and execution. Every good plan has to have a timeline and the courage to complete the goal. Throughout the chapters, you'll learn more about each *Stratechic* step and a recommended deadline to ensure constant progression. Using milestones and having a pre-determined timetable has served me well as a media executive, wife, mother, and change agent. Overcoming obstacles and enjoying success were all possible through development and application of these steps.

Timeline Exercise (30 minutes):

You won't know where to go unless you know where you've been. Creating a timeline helps map-out a path forward and humble your walk in the process. Take 30 minutes to create your timeline. During this exercise, I ask that you be extremely thoughtful and factual about where you've spent your life. I recommend doing it in one, five or ten year blocks. This gives you enough of a picture to see where time has been well spent versus wasted and clarifies your path forward.

stratēchic

Here is an Example of My Personal Timeline:

My Personal Timeline

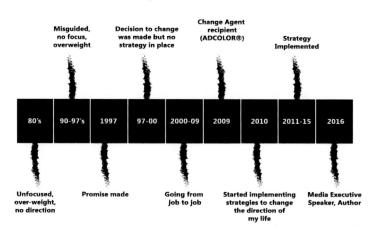

Misguided, no focus, overweight

Decision to change was made but no strategy in place

Change Agent recipient (ADCOLOR®)

Strategy Implemented

| 80's | 90-97's | 1997 | 97-00 | 2000-09 | 2009 | 2010 | 2011-15 | 2016 |

Unfocused, over-weight, no direction

Promise made

Going from job to job

Started implementing strategies to change the direction of my life

Media Executive Speaker, Author

By now, you should have evaluated the best thing that's ever happened to you and created your timeline. Both of these are considered 'awareness tactics' with the primary function of driving motivation. For many of you, you'll complete the two exercises and quickly see how much of your lives have been spent focused on the wants and needs of others. My desire is for you to now say, "the best thing that happens to me will be for and about me!" The exercise also helps you put your life into perspective. The past is just that. It's a reflection of what has happened but it doesn't have to be a mirror to what will be.

The next 10 chapters will be spent encouraging you to do something for yourself now that you are acutely aware of the time you may have wasted. It is time to develop a plan for your life. This book will guide you to become a Stratechic and transform your life into the woman God created!

Time Allocation Exercise: (2 hours)

Before jumping into the 10 Stratechic steps, I need you to complete one last exercise. Let's evaluate how we spend most of our time. This will be very important because without the appropriate time allocation, you can't make anything happen.

I want you to create a pie chart or a graph showing how you spend most of your time in a typical day.

Here is an Example of My Typical Day:

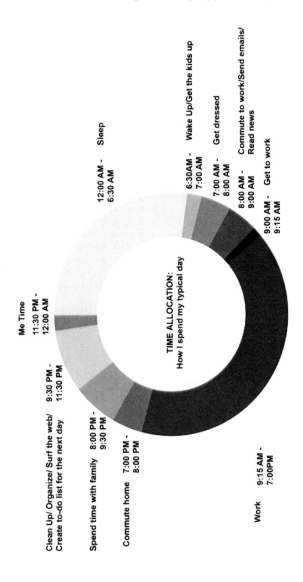

TIME ALLOCATION:
How I spend my typical day

12:00 AM - Sleep
6:30 AM

6:30AM - Wake Up/Get the kids up
7:00 AM

7:00 AM - Get dressed
8:00 AM

8:00 AM - Commute to work/Send emails/
9:00 AM Read news

9:00 AM - Get to work
9:15 AM

Work 9:15 AM -
7:00PM

Commute home 7:00 PM -
8:00 PM

Spend time with family 8:00 PM -
9:30 PM

Clean Up/ Organize/ Surf the web/ 9:30 PM -
Create to-do list for the next day 11:30 PM

Me Time 11:30 PM -
12:00 AM

How can you build or change anything with a schedule like this? Something has to give. It takes extreme discipline and focus. When I decided to write this book, I made a commitment to spend at least one hour, four nights a week writing as well as every time I stepped onto an airplane.

When I decided to get in shape, I left work at 6:15PM instead of 7PM and went to the gym for 45 minutes, 3 nights a week. All of the above requires awareness about how your current time is spent and the focus to make changes based on your current needs. My experience has taught me that if we carve out just 1 hour for ourselves each day, we can make miracles happen. Your wheel will look different based on your seasonal goals.

Stratechic Rule #1

SELF-AWARENESS IS NON-NEGOTIABLE
(90 DAYS)

"Knowing yourself is the beginning of all wisdom"
-Aristotle

Self-awareness is a clear understanding of your personality and "how others perceive you." It is an essential tool for successful leadership and a trait all good managers should strive to attain.[2]

Self-awareness is critical whether you are 18 years old and just beginning, reinventing yourself at age 50, or any age in between. It is the first step to becoming Stratechic. Remember, a Stratechic uses her female traits to create the perfect plan for her life and then executes like only a woman can.

This chapter forces you to not only look in the mirror, but also at your surroundings. Not everyone is prepared to be honest about what they see staring back. Until you are ready for the truth and decide to take action to improve your current situation, you don't need to read this book. Give it to a friend that has the potential for greatness.

There are two goals for this chapter. The first is to understand who you are today. Once you have an understanding of who you are (whether you like that person or not), that will allow you to pay attention to your surroundings. Then you will begin to understand how others see you. Both of these are integral to success.

Why Self-Awareness is Important

There was a young lady who came to me for advice. She wanted to know why she was not getting promoted. I knew she was very smart and capable because she had helped me with several projects. She sat in my office wearing too much makeup and a very tight dress that showed way too much cleavage. Most people will never tell us the truth, even when we ask. We worked for a very conservative company. I was sitting there thinking, 'she has no self-awareness.' She had no idea who she was or how her environment (peers and leaders) viewed her. It was fatal. Unfortunately, she never got promoted and finally left the company.

A survey of 75 members of the Stanford Graduate School of Business Advisory Council rated self-awareness as the most important competency for leaders to develop.[3] Leaders who foster self-awareness develop tools for leveraging their strengths and confronting their weaknesses. They earn credibility and cultivate relationships based on trust and respect. In addition, they remain open to new ideas, inquiry, and constructive criticism.[4] This is applicable to all women whether you are a CEO, self-employed, schoolteacher, or stay-at-home mom. It runs the female spectrum.

Research by Hay Group, culled from its 17,000-person behavioral competency database in 2012, found that when it comes to empathy, influence, and the ability to manage conflicts at the executive level, women show more skill than men. Specifically, women are more likely to show empathy as a strength, demonstrate strong ability in conflict management, show skills in influence, and have a sense of self-awareness.[5] Roughly half of the women in the Women & Strategy Study proactively seek feedback about strengths & weaknesses once a month or more. 80% proactively seek it at least once a quarter.

When was the last time you took a real assessment of yourself? Ask yourself the following questions: Who am I? What are people's perceptions of me? Those questions all lead to who I am currently, who do I want to be and how do I want people to see me. That's fairly easy to say but much harder to uncover, especially since we've been told over and over again that you shouldn't care what other people think. That's partially true. You can't win unless you know what others think— not knowing puts you at a disadvantage. The winner of the game understands that you can't give energy to the process. I don't own what people think of me; I own having the knowledge so I can leverage that knowledge to my benefit. Knowledge is definitely power!

What did I do to go from an uneducated, unemployed, overweight young lady with no vision BUT who had great potential? I listened to that small voice that said, "Do better." Today, I am whispering to you, no matter where you are, you can do better. You can be better. It absolutely begins with self-reflection.

My transformation took sacrifice, honesty and a commitment to a bigger goal. Let's begin to outline the steps. At 26, I did not have a college degree, lived at home with my dad, had low self-esteem, and was thirty pounds overweight. The first thing I did was spend time self-reflecting. I actually wrote it down. What do I enjoy? What makes me happy? What do I not like about myself? Then I wrote down very personal attributes. Do I smile or frown? Do I slump or sit up straight? Do I have a firm or limp handshake? Do I have a positive attitude? Do I speak to people when I'm walking down the street? How do I feel when a homeless person asks for money? You can't change until you acknowledge and accept who you are.

Next, I noted the characteristics I liked and did not like. I took this information and began to change my attitudes and behaviors. The bottom line is that I did not think about how someone else would've written my list nor did I discuss my answers with others. I actually got a pen and paper and wrote it out. I began to pay attention to how people treated and reacted to me. It is amazing what we learn when we focus. I uncovered that people would stare at me in different situations. They would   pay attention when I spoke. I realized that I was a people person. When I smiled at people and said good morning, most spoke back to me. I became happier and more confident.

To move my station in life, I had to make some changes. For example, my first big deficiency was a lack of education. Many jobs today use education to filter candidates. I had done well in school but knew I had to go back to advance my life and career. I had no idea what I wanted to do for a living but I knew I needed options. You have to understand the barriers in your life and make the necessary plans to change them. What are your barriers? What's holding you back?

I enrolled in school and got a part-time job. It was better to earn a small amount of money than to be in a bad relationship and not feel good about myself. Because of my late start, I didn't graduate until I was 30 years old. When I finally graduated, I was able to get a job, not my dream job, but a good job.

Always remember that self-awareness is a continuous process. That job was in Finance. Although it wasn't my dream job, it was a far cry from cleaning houses and working at the front desk of a hotel. Mind you, both of those jobs are respectable, however, I knew I was working beneath my ability. We've all been there. My job in Finance paid more but still wasn't fulfilling.

The second and maybe more important aspect of self-awareness also allows you to understand who is not in your corner. I lived in New York for three years and was really excited about interviewing for a new job at a reputable entertainment network. The job would be a big step in terms of responsibility and compensation. After several interviews, I was asked to supply the hiring manager with three references. I was confident in asking three of my best clients to vouch for me if called about the opportunity. At the end of the process, I was offered the job and had a very successful career at that network. I still keep in touch with the gentleman who hired me. We went out to lunch a couple of years ago (both of us had left the network). We were catching up and reminiscing. He looked at me and said, "Michele, remember when I hired you? I hired you despite receiving a really bad referral from one of the clients you listed as a reference." I was shocked. I mean, really shocked. I had vetted my referrals and actually spoke to them prior to including them on my application. Had I invoked self-awareness, I would have never listed a person who had been nothing more than cordial to me. I didn't read the signs. It was a huge lesson and that has never happened again.

What's sad is that sometimes people will try to block your success for no apparent reason. My old approach to people who did not like me (or, as I affectionately call them, "haters") was screw them. Through maturity and growth in my faith, I realized that enemies take too much energy. Did I just quote Drake? LOL! I won't allow anyone to distract me from my mission to reach my full potential. The worst thing is to let someone bring out a bad attitude. It carries a stigma over your head for a long time and might prevent you from getting what is rightfully yours.

So how do you shake that gut feeling that you're selling out or being disrespected when you speak to someone you absolutely know has no good intentions for you? You ask yourself, why do they dislike me? Why are they blocking me? The answer doesn't matter when I know that every roadblock I have ever encountered was blocking me from something great. Now, when there aren't adversaries, I start to get worried that progress isn't being made.

Before my dad passed away, he told me that if I don't have enemies, blockers, or haters, I'm not doing enough. I'm not successful enough. I've seen so many people angry and mad because they aren't getting what they want at work, school or in a relationship. They are not aware enough to know that they have now given people a valid reason to never elevate them. She has a bad attitude. She's not a team player. She's emotional (don't you love that one?). Oh, and my favorite, she's angry. Yes, you have a reason to be all of those things but the trick is you can't let anyone see it. Ever! There's a different set of rules for women and emotional displays are a huge excuse for people to put women in a no-progress/no-promotion bucket.

Self-awareness, the first **Stratechic** step, is time-consuming but essential. With it, you can evaluate where you are and where you want to go. That clarity will expose your abilities and shortcomings and allow you to understand how to stratechically manage your daily interactions and personal relationships to your benefit.

Self-Awareness Checklist (2 hours):

What are my best qualities?

What adjectives describe me?

What do people think of me? How do I know?

Ask people "how am I doing" at work, school, and home?

How can I improve?

Who can I confidently add to my reference list?

Who do I want to be?

What steps can I take to get there?

How long will it take (be realistic)?

Who are the people that can help me get there?

Who is on my enemy watch list?

Stratechic Rule #2

TRANSFORM YOUR CIRCLE: BUILDING YOUR VILLAGE (180 DAYS)

*I have always known that if you want to be
successful at anything you do in life, you have
to surround yourself with the people that are good
at it. Training with champions makes you one.*
-Nik Lentz

It takes a village. "Surround yourself with people who can continually tell you the truth about yourself! They may not be praying for you but you are absolutely positive they aren't praying against you."

Before my father passed away, he shared many important lessons. I remember him laying in the hospital bed just staring at me. When he finally spoke he said, "Baby girl, you can't take everyone on your journey. Everyone can't go!" At the time, I didn't know what he meant. Of course, I had to learn the hard way. I trusted people with too much access and too much information. Just as people often play a pivotal role in your success, they can also contribute to your failure.

Currently, I have the greatest seven friends on Earth. I have elected to keep my circle tight—very tight. I don't question sharing sensitive information with them because they are all trustworthy. For reference, I don't use the term 'friend' lightly. I remember sitting in a Girl Scouts meeting and the leader was teaching the girls how to resolve conflict with new friends. She repeatedly used the term 'friend'. I politely raised my hand and made a recommendation to not use the word friend so freely. It's more likely the girls will have to resolve conflict with acquaintances, not friends. The process is very different.

Every woman has to go through her closet and do some cleaning in preparation for a new season. The same goes for the new season you are going to walk into when you apply the principles in this book. You need to clean out your proverbial friend, acquaintance, and relationship closet. As we work on becoming self-aware, people who have our best interest (and not) become clear. My counselor in college would always say, "When someone shows you who they are – believe them because they've known themselves a lot longer than you have." We've all been disappointed and maybe even betrayed (I call it played). The point is to begin to identify people who aren't on your team and remove them. Period!

Let's get **Stratechic** with how you will build your team. First, create a personal board of directors that consists of the following: a chairman of the board, an advocate, an advisor and a sponsor.

Why didn't I mention mentors? I believe mentor relationships are a dying breed. They require a greater time commitment and a deeper level of trust. I'm not saying mentors can't be valuable. However, there are other options available to help you achieve your desired outcome. Advocates, advisors, and sponsors are just as effective in most cases and less time-consuming. I receive many requests from people who want me to mentor them and I just don't have the time to allocate to the commitment. However, I can advise, advocate, or sponsor for them. This can and has been just as valuable and influential.

Your board of directors may be different as you pass through different phases in life. In college, your board probably includes your parents, a teacher and a friend.

If you are in Corporate America, your board should consist of a friend/confidant, a peer in the same industry, a leader in the company, an influencer in your line of work and someone who is an influencer in the community.

An entrepreneur's board should consist of people in their line of work, similar companies, a close friend, a lawyer, a financial expert and other entrepreneurs.

I have to mention influencers. I love the word influencers. They aren't dictated by title or position. Get to know who the real influencers are in your company, school, church, etc. It's important to know the HR team and every administrative assistant in your department. People can't get to me if they are rude to Brittney. Her title of Executive Assistant doesn't describe her influence. I would also recommend that you know who pays you and how you get paid.

Building Your Team: Cleaning out your "Relationship" Closet (Continuous):

Over the next 30 days recruit the following team members:

Advisors: someone who can give direction and advice. This person needs to be in a position of knowledge about the subject matter.

Advocates: someone who has a seat at the table. This is the person who will put you on a list for promotion and make sure they pick you for assignments that will help you grow.

Sponsors: someone who has the power to write checks on your behalf and recommend you for jobs and assignments. They see you through the process to completion.

Leave behind list: who are the people that you know will not fit during the next phase of your life? People that get a lot from you while never giving anything back? They don't help you grow and want you to believe that you've already arrived. They don't push you to be better.

Social Media clean-up: Every six months you should clean up your Facebook page, especially since it is common for individuals and businesses to use social media as a resource to gather information about potential employees, vendors, etc. Your social media presence is an extension of your resume. Sometimes 'friends' and connections may post information that you wouldn't want associated with your personal or professional brand. Just as we manage our connections in real life, we have to do the same online. The good news is that there are applications to remove posts and unwanted comments. They also have apps that can clean up your account and Friends list based on word searches.

Here are some simple guidelines to follow when it comes to social friends and online connections:

Don't have friends on Facebook that you wouldn't bring to an interview or dinner with your grandmother. Never put in writing what you wouldn't want to share with your co-workers or family. Don't post any pictures you wouldn't want printed and hung in the hallways of your job or children's school. Your social media profile is your resume and bio. It is considered with your children's school application. It's even part of the sourcing for new credit or big purchases. Surprisingly, I've had people Google me while I was in the process of making a purchase.

My son and daughter were goofing around at our friend's house and their daughter videotaped them. My daughter shared the video saying, "Mommy, look how funny!" I politely asked her who filmed the video. She tells me her friend filmed it. I explained to both my children to never allow someone to videotape them even when they are just goofing around. They should always own their own content. It's a big lesson for little kids but it is NEVER too early to learn that they have to be in control of their images whenever possible.

Stratechic Rule #3

RELATIONSHIPS ARE CRITICAL
"NETWORKING AT ITS BEST"
(120 DAYS)

If you want to go fast, go alone.
If you want to go far, go together.
- African Proverb

People are always asking how have I been able to build great relationships at work and in my personal life. Let me just say for the record that not everyone is a fan of Michele Thornton. I accept that truth because I know I walk with several key attributes all the time: transparency, authenticity and integrity. People like to say that I keep it real. Why are these important qualities when building relationships? I've found people respect others that can be honest even when it won't benefit them. I always walk in my authentic self. Of course, I will tone it down if the environment is somewhat conservative but I never turn it off completely. Never. People can tell when you aren't being your true self. They feel they can't trust you.

Building great relationships requires planning and preparation. Why do people come to events and not have an idea of the speakers, the agenda, or what they want to accomplish? They don't have a plan for their time spent. The key to networking is preparation and follow-up. Before I go to any event, I research the topics and the panelists. I make sure I set a clear agenda on what I want   to accomplish and with whom I want to meet. A Stratechic makes contact with the person she would like to speak with a week before the scheduled event. You become memorable and have an instant conversation starter with the person. It seems quite simple but most people don't do it.

I was speaking at an event in 2014 and a young lady sent me a message via LinkedIn. She asked to meet me before or after the event and introduced herself. She gave a description of what she looked like and told me she would be wearing a pink dress. When I arrived at the event, I was actually looking for her. Impressive!

Scott Allen says, "Whether you're attending a weekly networking breakfast or an annual tradeshow, planning for a networking event will help you get the most out of that precious little amount of face-to-face time that you get to spend with other business professionals."

Proper preparation consists of:

Knowing who's in the room and preparing to meet those who seem to be a particularly good contact for you (or you for them).

Preparing to make a good first impression. That includes understanding the dress code. I love fashion and expressing myself through clothes. I make sure I know the environment and dress accordingly.

Plan ahead to be stress-free, in a good mood, and arrive in a timely manner.[6]

Stratechic Networking Tips

Business Cards:

When I get someone's business card, I jot down notes on the card to remind me of the person. I usually write down what they have on or a unique characteristic. I also place an X if I should follow-up with them. I then scan their business card into my cell phone using the Evernote app.

Follow-up:

Make sure you follow-up within 48 hours of meeting them. Key point: DO NOT send a thank you email that includes a request or with your resume attached (unless they requested it). One of my biggest pet peeves is when I meet someone at an event, they ask for my card and they send a thank you/great to meet you note with their resume attached. The delete button is pushed faster than a roach scuttles when the lights come on.

If you are trying to build a relationship, send a thank you note and some relevant information they can use. Maybe it's an article about their business or information about a charity they support. If you do your research, you can find out so much about an individual.

Handshake:

A Fortune 500 CEO once said that when he had to choose between two candidates with similar qualifications, he gave the position to the candidate with the better handshake.

Extreme? Perhaps, but he's actually not alone in his judgment. While analyzing interactions in job interviews, management experts at the University of Iowa declared handshakes "more important than agreeableness, conscientiousness, or emotional stability." Seven other studies have shown that a handshake can improve the quality of an interaction, producing a higher degree of intimacy and trust within a matter of seconds, says "The Daily Muse Editor."[7]

A woman's handshake must be firm but not over-powering. Isn't it amazing that we have to pay attention to every detail? The good news is that we are built to pay attention, adjust and self correct when we need to get better. When shaking someone's hand, face them and look directly at them. Make the person feel as though there is no one else in the room.

Three out of four (74%) women believe networking has been crucial to their overall success. When I started working for a small independent cable network 15 years ago, I remember sending emails and calling people with no answer or returned calls. I had to get creative. I made an investment in custom stationary. I started sending handwritten notes via FedEx with a cute slogan or saying. I would end the note saying, "Isn't this effort at least worth a returned call?" Customize your email with an interesting eye-catching subject line and a great signoff/signature. Make sure you follow-up every couple of months to check in. Consistency wins in building strong relationships. Plus, it ensures you stay top of mind!

Another tip is to identify what charities or community organizations people support. This is a great way to get involved in something that is meaningful to the people you are trying to win over. Years ago, I heard about a really phenomenal organization that helps aspiring, diverse filmmakers (The Ghetto Film School). The President of our department was heavily involved with the organization. I knew it would be a win-win to volunteer. I'm a huge advocate of giving back to my community, encouraging more faces behind the camera that are from diverse backgrounds and it would also mean building a relationship with an influencer in the company. I served on that board for many years and still today call that executive my friend. He was instrumental in advancing my career and helping me create a very successful multicultural business at the company. I have to remind you that this strategy only works when you are authentic in your service.

Relationships have been the cornerstone to every promotion, career move, community service project, relationship at my children's school, and all the good things that matter in my life and career.

Stratechic Rule #4

ASK FOR WHAT YOU'VE EARNED
IF YOU DON'T ASK, SOMEONE ELSE WILL
(90 DAYS)

"Ask and it will be given to you; seek and you will find;
knock and the door will be opened to you."
–Matthew 7:7 NIV

This chapter is about getting your power back. It's about holding people accountable when we don't get what we've earned. I've seen people promoted or praised for being average. It's the most frustrating thing in the world when you aren't getting the recognition through promotion or compensation and you have no idea why. When we don't know where we stand, why don't we just ask the question?

I worked for a well-respected network for several years. I was not getting promoted although I had performed at a very high level. I served on various committees and even created a new business segment at the company that generated millions of dollars. I thought about the best way for me to position myself for promotion. Sometimes you have to take risks and be prepared to leave, ask tough questions and then be prepared for the answer. I made an appointment with a top executive in the company who could absolutely make sure my promotion came to fruition. We had a strong relationship and I confidently believed he recognized me as a valuable contributor.

Unfortunately, like most executives, he was busy and my promotion was on a list of 500 other necessary tasks he had to complete to run his department. How did I move my promotion up to the top of his priority list? I requested a meeting and asked him a couple of simple question: Was I doing a good job? Was I valuable to the company?

Did he want me to stay? He said, "yes" to each of my questions. Then I came with the unexpected. I asked him if the company wasn't willing to promote me, would he help me find employment elsewhere? My closing line was that I had earned the right to ask him for help and support even if that meant leaving. I was promoted within the year. It's understandable to be afraid but you have to ask for what you've earned. 96% of the Women & Strategy Research Study participants have had a professional experience where they asked for what they wanted even though they were afraid of the response. Of those that have asked for what they wanted even though they were afraid, 9 out of 10 had the situation work out either somewhat or completely in their favor. Of the small percent that didn't have it work out in their favor, they still don't regret asking.

There was another young lady who came to me to help her devise a strategy to get promoted. She had been an assistant for five years and had performed beyond her capabilities. She just wasn't getting promoted. Once I heard all of the details and analyzed her reporting structure, I believe she wasn't promoted because she would leave work at her scheduled time (not early) to get home so she could see her children before they went to sleep. She did this a couple times a week. They questioned her commitment to her job and worried that if she was promoted, she wouldn't be committed. Sounds absolutely ridiculous, doesn't it? I advised her to ask her supervisor what were the three things she needed to do over the next six months to get promoted. Once you have the criteria in writing, you can devise a plan to execute your strategy. She immediately sent a recap of their conversation to her manager. She now had the plan in writing. She created a timeline against the action plan. I told her to send an email once a month about her activity against the goals and how she was doing to her boss and copy the division head. I also recommended she have her peers and people she supported send an update about her progress. She stored the feedback and when it was time for her six-month review, she was ready to ask for her promotion and validate why she had earned it. She produced the written criteria that her manager had provided, the monthly progress reports, support from her peers and the individuals she supported, and me supervising the process from the wings. She was promoted and was one of the best Planners in the company.

This strategy also works in your personal relationships. There have been many times I've been in relationships and had to ask the question what are your intentions and what's the timing to make it happen. You may not like the answer but at least you know where you stand. If we don't ask, we don't get.

Ask For What You've Earned Exercise (1 Hour):

- Why have you not asked for what you've earned?

- Who can give you what you want?

- Know the obstacles and list them.

- Make an appointment to speak with the appropriate person.

- Ask what are the criteria to get to the next level.

- Set a timeline before you leave the meeting.

- Document and send a recap to the manager.

- Provide monthly, written follow-up around your progress against the list/expectations.

- Gather peer support.

- Follow-up and ask for what you've earned!

- Be prepared to leave if you are not going to get what you've earned within your designated timeframe (professionally and personally)

Strategic Rule #5

TURN UP YOUR SOCIAL GAME
(30 DAYS AND BEYOND)

*Social media is the ultimate equalizer. It gives a voice
and a platform to anyone willing to engage.*
- Amy Jo Martin

Social media has taken the world by storm. Whether you love it or hate it, social media is absolutely necessary. I would be lying if I said I was an expert. I'm not, but what I do know is that it's essential for you to have a strategy around your social media presence.

Because everyone needs to have a voice and presence socially, it isn't surprising that 74% of the Women & Strategy Study participants have a social media strategy and 81% use social media for their personal brand strategy. At minimum, most people have a presence on Facebook, Twitter, and/or LinkedIn. The question is what is your brand positioning on the different platforms? Most importantly, how do you keep up with the changing landscape?

The first recommendation is to define your goal for using social media. Is it purely social? Is it to communicate a message or build a brand? Once you've identified what you want to do, everything else will fall into place. You can decide what platforms to use, the image you want to portray, the messaging you will send, and how often you will communicate the message.

My goal is to create a social platform around the core pillars of being " Stratechic" and push those messages out as a reminder that women need to be **Stratechic** about the plans for her life so she can win.

That means I need to build a community of followers who can embrace these strategies and also motivate them to share the information with their followers. If I can build a village of supporters that have large followings, then my job becomes easier because I can leverage them to send out messaging for me. The content has to be relevant, compelling, and released on a weekly basis. Fortunately, I can choose to do it myself or I can hire a company to do it for me.

LinkedIn has been a great resource and a staple in my social media presence. I always keep my profile up to date. I monitor who views my page and I connect to important people that are in my long-term strategy. Also, I believe that the people I'm connected to have similar interests and are equally yoked. Through this platform, I've been able to connect with other professionals and source new job opportunities. LinkedIn will be a key tool for the Stratechic book launch.

LinkedIn should tell a story quickly and succinctly. Whether you have a descriptor or your actual title is really a preference. When someone sends me a request, I look at his or her title. Since that is important to me, I decided to list my title first. It's also vital to include all experience, including leadership in the community. I've been asked to speak and been approached for opportunities because of the leadership roles I've held outside of work. I also make sure that all of my information is up to date on all of my social media accounts including recent accomplishments and photos.

Key Note: Always have a contingency plan if you are ever locked out of your accounts or your data is lost. Make sure you can at least connect with the people you've identified as influencers, potential high-value connections, and personal or professional board members.

Every month, I Google myself to make sure nothing is posted that I did not or would not approve. Another suggestion is to set up Google alerts to monitor if your name is posted or mentioned. You can set up specific words, phrases or sites and get just-in-time updates whenever your name is mentioned.

One app I use daily to help organize my life is Evernote. It's a free application (you can choose to pay a small annual fee if you want more functionality) for your smartphone and computer and it will store anything. For example, I store my calendar for my children's school, PowerPoint presentations for meetings, important emails, articles to read, and to-do lists. The app also creates an email address for you so when you need to save an important email or presentation, you simply email the data to   your

Evernote email address. The best feature is the ability to sync between your computer, smartphone, or tablet. If you're not using Evernote to organize your life, you are really missing out!

Over the next 30 days, you should make a concerted effort to create or update your social media profile. Make sure your information is up to date including pictures, brand messaging, recent titles and accomplishments. People will look for you and through social media you have the ability to control how they perceive you and your brand. You should also have monthly check-ins to refresh your pages and ensure you are telling the most relevant and recent story for where you are at that point in your life and career.

Stratechic Social: Know your brand. Use a picture of yourself so people will know it's you. Keep your profile updated and build a village of followers and supporters who can send out messaging for you. Create a contingency plan if you are ever locked out (make sure you have important information). Search your name, set-up Google alerts, and monitor your mentions on a monthly basis.

Stratechic Rule #6

EXECUTE YOUR PLAN
(180 DAYS)

"A goal without a plan is just a wish"
-Antoine de Saint Exupery

"Vision without Execution is Hallucination"
-Thomas Jefferson

"The perfect plan, poorly executed, will fail. A lousy plan, well executed, is often successful. It may seem obvious, but the way to fix a failure is often simple: work harder."

-Scott H. Young, March 2009

This is one of the most important chapters in this book. The car without fuel can't go anywhere. The "E" is the gas in Stratechic. Execution is critical. So what are we executing? "Everything" that comes before and after the "E."

How many times have you attended a conference, church, weight loss session or company meeting and you get great advice? Once you get home, nothing changes. I mean nothing! We all know it's easy to hear great advice and strategy but very difficult to implement. Execution needs a few critical components: action, the desire to want something different, allocation of time, consistent follow through and a positive attitude.

You have to take action.

You have to want to change.

You have to carve out time to make it happen.

You have to follow-through with consistency.

When I decided to leave one of my previous employers because a promotion to manage people was not going to happen but critical in my growth, I began to execute a strategy to leave the company. Listen ladies, this happens to all of us. We hate our job, our relationship, or how we look in our cutest pair of jeans. The list goes on, but we don't know where to begin.

You begin at the beginning!

What are the steps I took when I decided to leave an employer that had no confidence in my leadership skills? I decided I was not going to continue to work at a place that didn't value my ability or accomplishments. I would rather put my energy into finding a new place of employment that would at least value my talent and leadership. The first thing I did was bought a white board and had it installed in my office. I made a physical list of the possible places I COULD work and another list of places I WANTED to work. I listed the people that could help me make my transition happen. It's amazing what becomes possible when you write out what you want and who can help you get there. I listed the things that were non-negotiable. I considered things like work-life balance, perks and benefits, opportunities to manage people, ability to grow within the company, and overall environment for success. I updated my resume and bio. I also made sure all of my latest accomplishments were listed in LinkedIn. I enlisted my board of directors and updated them on my options. I weighed the feedback they provided. I put a timeline against the move. Because I developed a strategy and executed against it, I found a great job.

This chapter is important for women because this is where we have to really make a commitment to make time for our life plan and ourselves. We execute plans for our children's birthdays, the PTA, retirement parties, holiday gatherings, summer camps, your pet's veterinarian appointment and then at the end of a long day, we spend 30 minutes thinking about us—what we want to do, what we want to accomplish. Time is to be valued and maximized. It is to be shared smartly.

I did the same thing when writing this book. To execute the completion of *Stratechic*, I had to identify the topic and a host of other variables, including how to edit and publish. I had to setup my LLC, figure how to promote and market the book and meet the timeline I set for myself. I implemented the same exact principles when I was looking for a new job. For you to be reading this book is a testament that the *Stratechic* framework works!

Stratechic Rule #7

CAPACITY TO CONQUER WHEN THINGS ARE CHALLENGING
(30 DAYS)

*"You never know yourself until the chips are down.
True strength is not measured when you're at your
strongest, but when you're at your weakest."*
-Rashad Evans

*"What people have the capacity to choose,
they have the ability to change."*
-Madeleine Albright

Research finds that men aren't as skilled as women at dealing with more than one problem or task at a time. One study found that women perform 70% better than men at juggling more than one task at a time.[8]

Capacity is the ability or power to do, experience, or understand something.

Capacity has two faces. The first is to work hard and smart. It's a given that you have to outwork and outperform your peers. Excellence is the best way to get exposure. Unfortunately, many of us know all too well that outworking your peers doesn't equate to the recognition, promotion or money you deserve. That is when the other side of capacity is crucial: the ability to endure the feelings that arise when you don't get what you deserve. To mask the feeling of disappoint and sometimes anger.

I've spent years playing the game, smiling when I witness average people promoted ahead of me. Instead of letting it get the best of me, I began to think about my options and devise a plan that would help me move up or move on. I became **Stratechic**.

So, how do you build capacity?

This is why self-awareness is so critical. You must know what makes you stressed and unfocused. You also have to know what motivates you. This is where a vision board becomes essential. Your vision board is a reminder of all of the things you want to do. It's a compilation of your goals and dreams that you are motivated to make a reality. This board should be placed in a visible place as a constant reminder that you have work to do.

Capacity comes from a desire deep within. Work ethic plays a role but not as much as wanting to send your kids to the school of your choice, or that new house with the pool in the yard or like me, a black Porsche 911 Turbo that I'm going to buy for my next birthday.

Let's get **Stratechic**!

Capacity becomes key when you aren't happy with your current situation. When you aren't getting promoted, can't find a job, or your significant other isn't cooperating. Capacity allows you to stay focused when you're in the valley and reminds you to never let people see you sweat. I advise people to always live and leave on their own terms.

When I was considering switching companies, I made sure no one knew how I felt. My attitude, work ethic and delivery never wavered. Why is this important? I could continue to contribute to my current job and that kept my skill level on par but also allowed me to leverage my resignation. I left on great terms and to this day, have a great reputation with my prior employers. Of course, I didn't always have this mentality. There were times that I wanted to walk in the door to a job and curse everyone out. You know the feeling. You've probably daydreamed about walking into a job and telling everyone about themselves and then quitting. **Stratechics** feel that way but never let it show. They use that energy or desire to fuel their next move.

Of all the women that have passed through my office, this is the number one topic discussed. They are angry, disappointed, or frustrated and they let it show. The stigma of a bad attitude is difficult to shake. Once you have the reputation, more times than not, you literally have to leave and start over. Don't let anyone or any situation put you in a position of weakness.

A few years ago, a young lady wanted to meet with me to ask me to help her get promoted. I really liked her and wanted to help. I knew I needed to have a tough conversation with her because she had a reputation of having a bad attitude. I'm really sensitive when it comes to this label. I know it's often given out unfairly. She was thoroughly frustrated, having been with the company several years and not advancing. Unfortunately, the young lady allowed the frustration to show in her attitude. I explained that she had to turn around the perception and advised her to implement the capacity strategy. Unfortunately, she just wasn't able to get over her anger and frustration and wasn't willing to play the game to get ahead. She didn't get promoted.

The end game is to continue to exercise capacity when things are not going your way.

Strategic Rule #8

HELP OTHERS: SERVE YOUR WAY FORWARD (60 DAYS)

*An intricate harmony between doing what you love
and doing it with meaning and direction."*
-Brittney Dorsette

No person was ever honored for what he received.
Honor has been the reward for what he gave.
— President Calvin Coolidge

I love the saying, 'Leadership is not created in the hallways of Corporate America but what you do outside of those walls.'

When I wasn't given an opportunity to lead people at work, I was able to build those skills on various boards and organizations where I volunteered. I was able to implement strategies and direct people to an end result.

My grandmother always told me that if I give from an authentic place, it's okay to get something out of my sincere generosity. That does not mean you should give to get. It means to be smart about where you spend your time, money and energy.

Looking back, it was illogical that one of my early employers, for whom I worked for several years and won numerous awards (internally and externally), wouldn't promote me to Vice President because the company didn't believe I could lead people. To this day, I have no idea how they came to that conclusion. What was the basis for that rationale? I assume they weren't convinced I could have direct reports that would accept my leadership and follow my direction. It's like getting a credit card; you can't get one until you have one.

Through community organizations and my board participation, I was enabled to lead and manage people. I also led task forces and advisory boards. I chaired an important diversity organization. I was leading and leading and leading. All of that service, my sacrifice, was placed directly on my resume under the section called LEADERSHIP!

I won't hire someone that doesn't have some kind of community service listed because I know what skills you must have in order to serve the community; the passion it takes and the humility that's built in giving back.

At the end of the day, it's not about what you have or even what you've accomplished... It's about who you've lifted up, who you've made better. It's about what you've given back.
– Denzel Washington

I've built some very valuable relationships from serving on boards and working in the community. Those experiences introduced me to people that have helped me in my career and taught me invaluable skills. Including my previous boss, whom I served with on the board of Ghetto Film School. I've also met some great employment candidates through service.

Stratechic Rule #9

INVEST IN YOURSELF
(1 YEAR)

"Excellence is not a skill. It's an attitude."
-Ralph Marston

This is a big chapter for me. I make some admissions in this part of the book that I would have never made until I began to become self-aware. I needed to understand that I could reflect God's best image—but that it would take work, commitment, and sacrifice. I was overweight. I had low self-esteem. I tried to be cool and fit in with the in-crowd. I wanted the most popular man because that made me look better or be more accepted. I did things for people to be loved. Basically, I was a mess.

I talked about my dad and how his death was a catalyst for me wanting to be better, but I also have an aunt that I've looked up to for many years. She is a magnificent and brilliant human being. I never really tapped into her bank of knowledge, but I remember hearing her speak and her words stuck with me. Her huge shadow pushed me to want better until this day.

I was probably 18 years old and my aunt, Dr. Shirley Thornton (Colonel Thornton to those who know her through her military service), was being honored. In her speech, she said, "When I would walk into a room, they would first see that I'm black, then a woman, then I'm educated." Never forget that order. Women are more times than not judged visually and have to prove why they should have a seat at the table. It's not far from the old saying that "pretty will open the door, but smarts will get a dinner invitation and beyond."

A **Stratechic** understands that she walks, talks and dresses for the job or role that she wants, not the one she currently holds.

So let's talk about my transition because it was long and tedious. I didn't wake up looking, speaking and dressing like an executive.

On my father's deathbed I made him a promise. I actually spoke the last words he would ever hear. I told him that he was my hero and that I would make him proud of me. I made a commitment that I would walk in my best self. I had already made so many changes about the people I dated and the friends I hung out with, but I needed to make some personal changes. I needed to polish my image. I spoke with an Oakland slang. I was overweight. I dressed to get attention from the wrong people. I wasn't confident in front of people I didn't know.

When I moved to New York in 2000, I decided that I needed to have New York polish, so I hired a voice and diction coach. The woman had to be in her late 80's. She was prim and proper woman that served tea and always wore her St. John suit when I arrived for my lessons. The first three lessons she had me say my name over and over and over again. She would tell me there is power in how you say your name "Michele Thornton." She would have me pronounce every syllable. That wasn't easy because of the "n" in Thornton. Yes, she taught me the importance of pronunciation, but the more valuable lesson was teaching me to have confidence when I introduced myself to anyone.

I also knew that I had to lose weight. My weight fluctuated for years. It went up and down based on my love life or happiness with life in general. It was ridiculous. I would go on eating binges and then try to diet. Everyone reading this book knows how easy it is to gain five pounds and how hard it is to lose it.

Remember, I moved to New York and made a promise to my father. My success as a sales professional was in part tied to my appearance. I can also confidently say that most women recognize that appearance plays a factor in their careers (see my research results in the appendix).

I set boundaries based on my current situation. I work in the entertainment business so I am able to express myself through more fashion forward trends. I've also worked in the business for 15 years and have a track record of success. When I worked at a conservative network, I was fashion forward but somewhat conservative in my style. I had conservative staples and pushed the limits with accessories. I love a leather coat and a pop of color.

We have to be honest with ourselves and make decisions based on our current environment. Self-awareness plays a big role in how we determine what success looks like. Conforming does not mean selling out. We have to compromise in how we show up mentally and physically. When I decided to work in the entertainment business, I knew I had to make some changes. I had already gone to my voice and diction coach to tone down my Oakland accent. I also needed to lose 30 pounds. That was not as easy as saying my name over and over again.

Anyone who has ever had to lose weight knows it is a commitment that takes complete sacrifice and a change in habits. People always ask me how did I lose 30 pounds and keep it off after two kids and 20 years? I found two pictures of what I wanted to look like and I carried them everywhere. One picture was of me when I was slim and the other was of one of my favorite African America models (a girl can and should dream). I implemented a 30-day challenge. If I could maintain healthy eating habits for 30 days, just maybe that would begin to become a habit. I stopped eating bread and drinking sodas. Then I began to substitute fruits (only before 2 PM) and vegetables for unhealthy carbs. I still ate brown rice and brown pasta. The most critical components in all of my weight loss efforts were reducing my portion size (I only used small plates for all my meals), setting a timeline against my 30-pound goal (1 year) and consistency. It goes without saying that I exercised a couple of times a week. I still use the 30-day rule to this day. I'm embarking on my 50th birthday and look and feel better than ever before.

For me to be successful, I have to look and sound like the ultimate professional. The point is that I was thoughtful and understood my environment and path to success.

I love the saying "dress and act like the job you want, not the one you currently have."

I see young people in my business and they are adamant about self-expressing themselves through hairstyles, clothing selections, jewelry and approach to business. The marketplace dictates the rules. We can follow them with a few minor exceptions or find a place of employment that will allow us to self-express without growth penalties.

Stratechic Rule #10

CRAFT YOUR STORY AND SELL IT!
(45 DAYS)

"I've learned that people will forget what you said, people will forget what you did, but people will never forget how you made them feel."
-Maya Angelou

As we head into the last chapter, let's hone in on our storytelling skills. I call this our elevator pitch. Your resume and bio are only part of the story. Social media tells another version of your story. The story we are going to focus on now is when you are standing in front of a person that can influence something you want.

Every Stratechic should be prepared to tell and sell her story. 78% of the women we surveyed have a personal elevator pitch. What is your elevator pitch? It's a small window of time to impress someone and succinctly tell them who you are and in some cases, what you want.

Below are my personal and professional elevator pitches:

Pitch for my brand: Stratechic

Stratechic is a guide that boldly encourages women to think like a woman, plan like a CEO and tap into the strategy she was born with!

My professional pitch: Media Executive

My name is Michele Thornton and I'm a corporateprenuer in the media and entertainment business with over 15 years of experience. I build unbreakable relationships, am knowledgeable about black culture, live authentically, treat people with respect and give back like I may one day need someone to give to me.

My elevator pitch is written down and I carry it everywhere I go. I practice it in the mirror or in front of my kids. I make sure that I can tell my story at the drop of a dime. Anytime. Anywhere. I update my elevator pitch as often as necessary.

The point of crafting your story allows you to sell anything you want, including yourself. Everyone needs to know how to sell as everything in our world is bought and sold. Let's take a quick glance at some important sales characteristics.

Liz Wendling says: Why do so many business women spend more time hoping or praying for sales rather than just learning to sell? Because the mere mention of the word sales brings up fear, dread and anxiety in the hearts of many!

In this fiercely competitive economy, every meeting, sales call and interaction with a potential customer is vital to the success of a business. Women must have strong tools in their toolbox to create a long-term sustainable business.

What women don't realize is that they were born to sell! Here are five key reasons women make great salespeople. [9]

We are excellent listeners.

Women have a natural ability to listen, which allows us to build trust and gain rapport. Listening for information and clues about the customer—their interest in our products, what's important to them, stories about their children or hobbies—helps with the selling process. Listen to not only what is said but also what's not said.

We tend to be empathetic.

Putting ourselves in the customer's shoes enables us to discover specific details about the customer and how our product or service can help. We find out what's most important to our potential customer, how we can solve their problems, and what features and benefits our product delivers to fit their unique needs. Women's tendency to express their emotions and decode others' emotions allows us to tune in more to a client's needs.

We have strong intuition.

A woman's intuition is considered her sixth sense. Women tend to depend more on it than men do. Women have gut feelings, great antennas, an inner voice, a little nudge that says whether or not to move forward. We can sense things about people and predict if a potential customer is a good fit. Tapping into the gift of intuition provides tremendous value in the sales process.

We multi-task well.

Women are often touted for their multitasking skills. Since we often don't have the opportunity to do just one thing at a time, we've learned to do many. Women can hear several things and have multiple conversations simultaneously. They can juggle complex business tasks, feed a baby and find lost keys — all without skipping a beat.

We are naturally good socializers.

Most women love to socialize, and they excel at building relationships. Women socialize differently than men because we consciously make time to nurture and grow our personal and professional relationships. We're nurturers by nature, and this gift serves us well in business.

Women have what it takes to be great at sales! Our strengths, nurturing style, passion and intuition, which were previously discounted in the business world, have now taken hold. We can use our natural talents, combined with a little training, to grow our businesses exponentially!

So, go ahead, ignite your self-confidence and come alive. The only limits to what you can achieve are self-imposed. Go sell![10]

No matter where you are or what you do for a living, you must learn how to sell. I use my expertise as a sales executive in every aspect of my life. Whether I'm selling Girl Scout cookies with (or for) my daughter, raising money for one of the charities I support, or trying to convince my husband where our family should go on vacation. Sales skills are activated just like superpowers. Women are born with the aforementioned characteristics. We need to embrace and use them to advance our strategies and plans.

I've been placed in many situations that had me pulling out my elevator pitch and scrambling to put my best foot forward. Selling and networking go hand in hand. Just like you have to be ready when you are at an event to meet the right people, you have to be ready with your story.

Great story telling is critical in closing a deal or getting a great seat at a restaurant. Roughly 90% of my day is spent selling. I may take that skillset a bit too far, but I know how important it is to get what I want. The bottom line is to be a good sales person; you have to be a good communicator.

There are a couple of things not mentioned that also make a great sales person. They ask questions and build meaningful relationships. Women are inherently inquisitive. Let's put that trait to good use in getting what we want.

At one point, I was working for the local phone company selling products and services to cities based in northern California. I was having a difficult time with one particular client. He accepted a meeting and during the meeting he kept shutting down all of the ideas I had to improve his business. So, I finally asked a question. Have you ever had a bad experience with this company? What he told me was shocking. The company had turned off his home phone over a very small discrepancy. Relief flooded over me. It's when you finally get to the bottom of a situation that you don't understand, which makes you feel like you just won a marathon. I asked him would he give me an opportunity to be his telephone service and equipment provider at work, if I could resolve his home situation? He said absolutely. The issue was solved in 24 hours and he became my biggest customer. I could have walked away just thinking we did not have the right product and services, but I felt it was more than that. Therefore, instincts play a big part in success but more importantly, it goes back to asking the right questions.

So, make sure you work on your sales skills: listen, ask questions, be empathetic, practice your story, work on your multitasking skills, keep and grow your relationships through truthfulness and authenticity, know the players, and use your intuition.

Bonus Chapter

KARMA: THE K IS NOT SEEN BUT HEARD (UNLIMITED)

"How people treat you is their karma;
how you react is yours."
-Wayne Dyer

Stratechic has a silent "K."

The last piece of our journey is to be acutely aware of Karma. As we implement our plans and make progress in our lives, we should commit to forgiving (not forgetting) the people that may have done us wrong, lied to/on us, hurt us, tried to block opportunities, not helped other women when they had the chance, and every other reprehensible thing in between! My grandmother would always tell me not to share good news until it was completely solidified. She didn't want anyone praying against me or sending out negative energy against my blessings.

Also, we must be dedicated to walking with integrity, treating people with respect, uplifting others when given the opportunity, helping the women that are worthy, and advising, advocating, and sponsoring other women on the rise. I had a young lady ask me why would I share my secrets to success? My answer was, "What God has for me, no one else can have." It's up to me to claim it. That's why I wrote this book, that's why I help so many women, that's why I advocate for others, so they can one day have a job in the media business, just like mine. I truly believe that because I walk with a spirit of giving, more is given to me. If you read this book and implement the strategies to become a **Stratechic** and not help others, all of your efforts will be in vain.

Congratulations ladies! You are well on your way to becoming *Stratechics*!

Stay focused, love yourself, and ***LET'S GO***!

stratēchic

Notes

1. Merriam Webster's Dictionary

2. Generator Group, July 16, 2013

3. Generator Group, July 16, 2013

4. Generator Group, July 16, 2013

5. Harvard Business Review, John Baldoni, May 9, 2013

6. Posted By Scott Allen- January 18, 2010, business.com

7. "The Daily Muse Editor."

8. Post published by Peggy Drexler Ph.D. on Aug 19, 2014 in Our Gender, Ourselves

9. Liz Wendling, Top 5 Reasons Women Make Great Sales People, August 4, 2010, Coloradbiz

10. Liz Wendling, Top 5 Reasons Women Make Great Sales People, August 4, 2010, Coloradbiz

APPENDIX

Women & Strategy Research Study Results

The *2015 Women & Strategy Research Study* was fielded via an online survey in October 2015 among 27 successful women ages 18-65. The women work across various industries and levels and represent every racial group. A summary of the study follows.

1. There were 3 common themes from the women's definition of "STRATEGIC":

    - Have clearly defined goals that you work toward

    - Have long-term vision and intentionally plan

    - Don't focus too much on the short-term

2. Roughly half of the women proactively seek feedback about strengths & weaknesses once a month or more. 80% proactively seek feedback at least once a quarter.

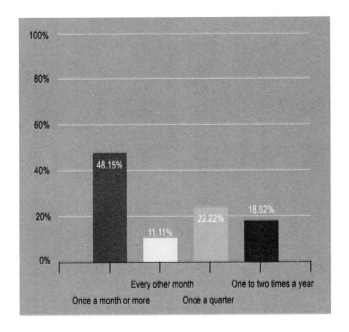

3. 96% of the women said self-awareness has played
    a crucial role in their personal and professional
    accomplishments. Of the tools they use to be
    more self-aware:

    - Over 96% use relationships with others
    - 89% use spiritual work/involvement
    - 85% solicit feedback directly

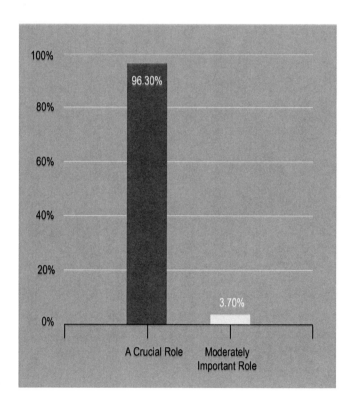

4. The women currently have a: (Note: participants were allowed to select multiple responses)
   - Sponsor 56%
   - Mentor 63%
   - Advocate 74%
   - Advisor 85%

5. Less than half (44%) of the women believe having a mentor was very important to their overall success.

6. Less than 4% of the women believe networking had little to no impact on their success. Three out of four (74%) believe networking was crucial to their overall success.

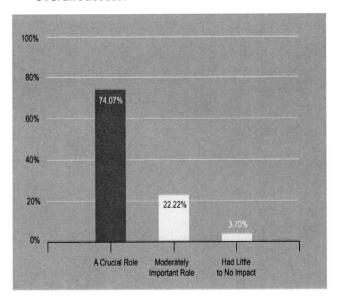

7. 67% of the women have a unique approach to networking. Of those women, they overwhelmingly list "relationship building" and "creating meaningful connections" as the secrets to their approach.

8. 78% of the women have a personal elevator pitch.

9. 59% believe their looks/appearance has played an important role in their success and career progression. 63% of the women have been in a position where they know their looks/ appearance enabled them to advance faster and 67% believe looks/appearance should be a factor in someone's success.

10. 96% have had a professional experience where they asked for what they wanted even though they were afraid of the response. Of the women that have asked for what they wanted even though they were afraid, 9 out of 10 had the situation work out either somewhat or completely in their favor. Of the small percent that didn't have it work out in their favor, they still don't regret asking.

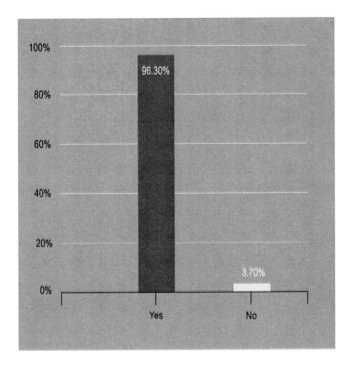

11. 93% of the women believe their professional career has given them access to their purpose as well as better define and translate it.

12. Roughly 1 out of 5 of the women allowed someone or something else to dictate their current roles while over 74% (3 out of 4) either created their current roles based on what they believed it should be or altered it to better fit their strengths and vision for the organization.

13. 74% have a social media strategy and 81% use social media for their personal brand strategy.

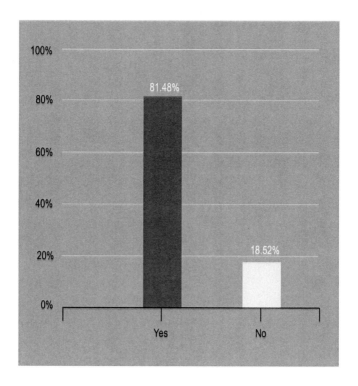

14. The women in the *2015 Women & Strategy Study* are mothers, business leaders, entrepreneurs, and artists.

JOB TYPE (SELECT ALL THAT APPLY)	
I am a Senior Executive at a large company	44%
I am an entrepreneur/business owner	52%
I am a consultant/freelancer/independent contractor	19%
I am a stay-at-home mom	4%
I am a middle manager	11%
I am an artist (writer, actor, musician, etc.)	15%

stratēchic

WE'D LOVE TO HEAR FROM YOU!

Post your review of **Stratechic** on Amazon, join the community at www.stratechic.com, and follow Michele on Twitter (@ThorntonMichele) and Instagram (@Stratechic)!